# THE PRISONER'S PRAYER BOOK

For Betty —
  My savior when it comes to
taxes! Like a deer in the
headlights.... Thank you!
Louise

# THE PRISONER'S PRAYER BOOK

### LOUISE ANN SIPES REICHERT

PRINCIPIA
MEDIA

The Prisoner's Prayer Book
Copyright © 2012 Louise Ann Sipes Reichert
All Rights Reserved

Published by Principia Media, LLC
Wyoming, MI
principiamedia.com

ISBN: 978-1-61485-302-5

Scripture taken from the NEW AMERICAN STANDARD BIBLE®,
Copyright © 1960,1962,1963,1968,1971,1972,1973,1975,1977,1995 by
The Lockman Foundation. Used by permission.

Cover Art: *Shackled* © 2011, FreeRayGray
Page 3: *Troubled Man* © 2011, Curtis L. Chase*
Page 33: *Beyond the Chains* © 2011, Troy Chapman
Page 53: *Shine, Jesus, Shine* © 2008, Troy L. Rienstra,
    Founder of Christians for Prisoners & Prisoners for Christ
Page 73: *Lord, Please Watch Over My Family* © 2011, FreeRayGray
Page 89: *Decisions to Come* © 2011, FreeRayGray
Page 105: *Sole Asylum* © 1999, Nancy Jean King*

    *Graciously provided by the Prison Creative Arts Project
    Ann Arbor, Michigan

Cover Design: Frank Gutbrod
Interior Layout: Della Landheer

Louise may be reached at...
email: 2inspire@chartermi.net
website: prisonersprayerbook.com

Printed in the United States of America

10 9 8 7 6 5 4 3 2 1

# Dedication

This book is dedicated to the men I met at Marquette Branch Prison who helped spark the idea of writing prayers, particularly to Steven Rodney Smith and Robert Kein for freely sharing their thoughts and feelings with me, and for giving me more of an "inside" look at life behind bars.

More importantly, this book is dedicated with great pride to my father, John Francis Sipes. Without his love and encouragement, I would never have become the person I am today. How I wish he could have lived to see me grow up, and how I wish we could have known each other for much longer than a mere fourteen years!

From the moment I first inquired about prison ministry, I believe the Spirit has been busily at work. My prison ministry experience was, in fact, for me, profound. It is my conviction that, no matter what our hopes, dreams, fears, or regrets might be, we are all bound by similar feelings, that permeate our lives. It is my prayer that that same quiet, but insistent Spirit work effectively in the lives of all those who read these prayers, providing comfort and relief to troubled souls everywhere.

*Louise Ann Sipes Reichert*

# Contents

# Contents

## Foreword
### Does Jesus care?

My friend David has given up on God. "Why should I keep on praying?" he asks. "He doesn't listen to me, anyway."

David is in prison for a crime he didn't commit, and he believes that if God answered prayer he would be out by now. He has confused the wrong answer with no answer. Claiming that this helps to prove his innocence, he points out that he could have accepted a plea bargain. David was offered a sentence of one year in a county jail in exchange for a guilty plea. He refused. He wouldn't accept the bargain because he would have had to plead guilty to a lesser charge, tantamount to admitting guilt. And he refused to admit that he committed the crime. So he ended being a very angry prisoner who served seventeen years behind bars.

I shared his story with Louise, and she immediately began writing. She knew David's thoughts:

> God, I'm pretty angry at You right now.
> Why are You allowing this to happen to me?
> I didn't do the crime that put me here.
> In fact, I don't think I did anything to deserve this!
> ("*So Angry*," page 11)

And that paved the way for this book. Louise is a friend and supporter of Humanity For Prisoners. When I learned that she skillfully pens prayers to match the needs and issues of prisoners, I kept encouraging her to write. I'd relate prisoner problems. She'd respond with prisoner prayers. In subsequent conversations, we decided that these petitions had to actually be seen and prayed by inmates. Praise God, the book is now a reality.

In my role as a church musician I was recently asked to accompany a singer who had chosen the old hymn "Does Jesus Care?" I hadn't thought of the hymn in years, but still remembered that as a teenager, when all little emotional bumps and bruises seemed like unsolvable crises, I would go to the piano and play it.

I've been thinking about that hymn a lot as Louise and I have been working on this project of offering a book of meaningful prayers that would relate to the needs of prisoners. Often I can hear the words of the hymn through the emotion in the voice of prisoners: "Does Jesus care when my heart is pained too deeply for mirth or song, as the burdens press, and the cares distress, and the way goes dreary and long?"

It is my goal to place a copy of *The Prisoner's Prayer Book* in the hands of every prisoner who wants one here in the State of Michigan and beyond. Thanks to these creations by Louise, we can say to those behind bars: "Oh yes, he cares, I know he cares, his heart is touched with your grief; when the days are weary, the long nights dreary, I know my Savior cares."

Yes, dear inmate, Jesus cares. So do we.

*Doug Tjapkes, Founder of Humanity For Prisoners*
*Author, Sweet Freedom*

# Preface

It is the author's hope that these "conversations" with God will appeal to prisoners because of the nature of their settings as well as their "raw" quality. *The Prisoner's Prayer Book*, reflects the author's conviction that we are all bound by similar feelings—only different circumstances. May those who read this book realize—no matter what their hopes, dreams, fears, or regrets might be—that God is with all of us and that He will provide comfort, if we simply allow Him into our lives.

# Acknowledgements

I would like to take this opportunity to especially thank Doug Tjapkes, author of *Sweet Freedom*, for his friendship, support and guidance, and mostly for believing in me. Thank you, too, to Della Landheer and Dirk Wierenga for their expertise, guidance, and faithful encouragement throughout the process. Without any one of you, this book may never have seen print. You are all awesome!

*Louise Ann Sipes Reichert*

# One

&

## We All Have Needs

*Troubled Man*
Artist, Curtis L. Chase

3

## Isolated

I called my mom today and got bad news.
My sister died a few weeks ago.
No one wanted to send me a letter with bad news,
So they waited until they heard from me.
Lord, I'm so isolated here!
It makes me angry, but then I realize
It was only I myself who put me here.
Lord, stop my anger.
Help me not to feel so all alone.
Could You just stay by my side today, Lord?
I'm scared…and lonely…and sad.
I need Your loving arms about me.

## A Home

I've always wanted to belong somewhere, Lord.
Didn't know my father 'cause he left when I was born.
Mom was hardly ever home.
Seems I always hung out with the wrong kids,
And I got in trouble early.
Once in awhile I'd find someone I especially liked,
But no one ever saw me for the real me.
I drifted—from drugs…to gangs…to jail…and then
I ended up here.
I haven't found a home yet, Lord.
My Christian friends tell me all that changes
When I claim You as my Savior.
Claim *me*, Lord, as Your own.
I'm longing for a home.

## A Single Touch

Lord, when I was on the outside, I never realized the
power of a single touch.

I remember holding my nephew…
He held my finger.
When my father died, my mother cried,
and I put my arms around her.
How good a hug would feel right now!
Heck, I would give anything
just to be able to hold someone's hand.

It is cold here, Lord, empty and cold.
Isolated, I have no one to love, or to love me.
I fight it, Lord, and try to remember
Just the good times…
but it's hard.

Touch me, Lord.
Remind me that You still love me.

## Youth Alone

I'm younger than most here, God.
I thought that older prisoners would help me out.
I thought they'd teach me the ropes.

Some have—just not the way I thought they would.
I thought that guards would have cared more, maybe
protected me more…but I think they take more
advantage of me because I'm young.

God, I've been teased, called names, and treated like dirt.
I've been hit, and jumped, and gassed.
I now know what sex abuse means.

There's not a safe place anywhere.
Only You, Lord, can keep me safe.
Help me, God.
I'm really scared.

## One More Day

Yesterday I fell.
I'm taking a new pill that makes me dizzy and
lightheaded.
A few prisoners were nearby, and a guard or two, but no-
body came to help me.
It was a scary feeling, and it reminded me of how alone
I am.

Jesus fell when He was being made to carry His cross.
No one helped Him, either.

How good it would have been to have someone
reach out, extend a hand, and help me to my feet!
I'm so afraid, Lord…and there is no one here who cares if
I live or die.

Strengthen me, Jesus.
Help me to make it…just one more day.

## Seg

They lock me in a cell for twenty-three hours each day.
I'm allowed one hour in an empty room to exercise—
Alone.
They say it's for my protection,
But God, I feel like they're out to get me.
Guards barely speak to me
And I have no privileges.
And there is no one to turn to
Except You, oh Lord.
Only You.
I cling by a thread
And hope and pray I will be strong enough
To hold on.

Keep me sane, Lord,
And stay with me,
For I am scared
And so, so alone.

## So Angry

God, I'm pretty angry at You right now.
Why are You allowing this to happen to me?
I didn't *do* the crime that put me here.
In fact, I don't think I did anything to deserve *this*!

People want me to be understanding, but this is my LIFE
—my life, which is slowly being sucked away each day
that I am here.

God, give me a reason to keep going, day after day.
Help me to see some reason within these walls
to explain why You have kept me here.

Show me, Father.
Show me.
I'm begging You.

## Raped

I raped a woman before I came here.
I hurt her a lot.
I forced her, and she fought me.
I couldn't stop myself
Until I paid her back for not wanting me.
She paid me back by sending me here.
And, here, it happened again.
This time, though, I was the victim.
They shamed me, and I couldn't move.
They tore my flesh and battered me senseless.
They left me for dead. I deserved it.
Lord, now I know what I did to that woman.
I took away her right to choose,
And I hurt her in anger.
Calm my rage.
Help me to respect others and control myself
Even when I don't agree.

## Empty Space

It seems I spend my life waiting, Lord.
I wait for my sentence to end.
I wait in the chow line,
For meds,
For supplies,
To see the doctor.
*God, I'm so tired of waiting!*
I feel useless and dull and life is an empty place.
Lord, I need to look forward to something.
Help me to be able to feel alive through all this
waiting.
Show me how to have a purpose here.
Lead me to a fuller life, Lord…
Then let me live that life only for You.

# Daily Grind

I sit at my desk, beads of sweat rolling down my face.
I hear the steady blast of large fans in the dayroom.
My own fan moves the air in my room much more
gently. The *ketunk, ketunk* of the ping pong ball is an
almost constant sound throughout the day and early
night. Monotonous sounds. Dull, just as my life behind
these walls. Each day, each night are always the same.

I know I must serve my time to pay for all the wrongs
I have done, but Lord, let me use this time for good.
Father, help me to see past the ordinary. Help me to
recognize Your hand at work—yes, even in this prison.
Help me to appreciate little things that I would otherwise not notice. Help me to take the time to stop to
help someone in need. Make me stop to listen to a
fellow prisoner who wants to talk.

Grant me eyes to see You in others, Lord, and ears
that hear You speak. Let my words be loving words.
Guide my feet to remain on the path that You have
set, oh Lord. Protect me from the evil that surrounds me.
Allow me, Lord, to live a life that is anything but ordinary.

## Arson

I've been drawn to fire
For as long as I can remember.
It dazzles. It hypnotizes.
It always seemed to take away
The bad feelings that came from
Being hit and made fun of.

Father, I don't always understand things
But I know You use fire
To get rid of things that are bad.
Father, burn away the bad in me,
But save the good…

And let *it* burn a longing in *me* for *You*.
With Your help, I can be a better person.

## Pedophile

Yes, Lord, they call me a pedophile.
It's a label I hate…but it's also true.
I was a victim years ago, and
I relive those events, over and over.
I try to make sense of it all.
I try to make the memories stop replaying in my head.
I try to find a way to take control of the situation,
And make it stop.
I can't let it go.
The docs don't know how to make it stop, either.
Given the chance, they say I will probably reoffend
Because I keep trying to make right what was done to
me.
I want to be able to stop.
I want to be able to stand up to what was done to me.
I want—for once—to get it right.
Lord, I would give anything for You to remove this
burden from me.
But I am damaged.
They say, Lord, that You hate the sin, yet love the sinner.
Then love me, Lord,
For I need so very much to be loved.

## Channel

Father, I long to give You service...but I'm imperfect and have so many needs. I want to bring meaning to the lives of others, yet I struggle with the meaning of life itself. I long to care and hope, yet arguing and fighting surround me. I can't help but be reminded of the prayer of St. Francis of Assisi to "make me a channel of Your peace."

Lord, I need You today. I need reassurance to know I'm loved by You. I need encouragement to press forward. Help me to realize I am worthy of Your love. Help me to put my desire for good into good deeds.

Let me be a parent today to someone who needs guidance. Let me be comfort to the lonely. Let words I say be the right words, and, yes Lord, may Your love shine through me today.

## Deeper

The days drag on, oh Lord, each day the same as the one before. Father, help me to see what is *not* usual in this weary world. Help me to see kindness, moments of hope, and encouragement. Then, if I am able, Lord, let me make those moments larger, and pass them on.

You have blessed me, Lord, with an ability to see beyond a first impression. When this happens, I always know it is Your light that shines in me. Allow me, Father, to be able to bring Your light into the life of some fellow prisoner's otherwise drab and lonely existence.

May I always look a little deeper for the good You always place within.

## Listening

I'm learning to listen.
When we're young, we (should) listen to our parents.
In school, we (should) listen to our teachers.
At work, we listen to bosses.

Lord, I'm learning more and more about You,
As well as about myself.
I'm learning that You always love us,
No matter what we've done.

But I'm stubborn and impatient, Lord.
When I ask You for something in prayer,
It's very hard to wait for an answer—
If I can even *hear* an answer.

Father, help me, in spite of my strong self will,
To be able to hear Your wishes for me.
Quiet *my* way, Lord, and open me to *Your* way.
I'm here, Lord. I'm listening.

## Addiction

Cravings.
It used to be I'd lie, cheat, and steal
Just to get a drink.
And when I came here,
The cravings continued.
I even learned how to ferment fruit to get high.
Over time, Lord, I learned about You.
At first, I wasn't ready to accept You.
But then, small things began changing for me.
When I made the connection
Between my wishes for the day
(which actually turned out to be prayers to You)
And how my day went,
I was hooked.
Now, Lord, I'm addicted to You.
May my craving for You remain in me the rest of my days.
Amen.

## Need

Father, I know the act of homosexuality is wrong,
Yet, I can now understand it.
I'm so lonely, Lord.
The hardest part about being in prison, God,
Is not being able to touch another human being.

Father, I see now how it happens.
We <u>need</u> to touch and to be touched.
We <u>need</u> to feel alive.

Lord, help me when I am tempted,
To think of You.
You touched others with kindness
…and fairness
…and love of one's spirit.

Teach me to touch others as You did, Lord,
And help me to think of others' needs
…before my own.

## Breakthrough

When I came here Father, I was angry—at family, at life,
at having gotten "caught."
I wasn't very nice to anyone, nor did I look for anyone to
be nice to me.

Over the years, though, that anger lessened.
I began to realize that not everyone wanted to hurt me.
It was new to have anyone reach out to me.
Some good Christians led me the rest of the way.

Now I can no longer shut people out,
And I like being a friend, helping where there's a need.
Father, open my heart to help those who push me away.
I know they really need someone because I, like them,
pushed others away.

Help me to break through that anger, Lord, and then…
Let me lead them to You.

## Parole Board

Dear Lord, I need a major helping of strength.
My parole board hearing is almost here.
I am nervous, anxious, and afraid.
God, help me to keep my cool, no matter what
they ask.
Let my answers be honest and my voice be
calm.

I have waited so very long for this.
If they deny me freedom, Lord, what then?
How will I keep going here?
Father, be with me.
See me through this ordeal.
I need You now more than ever before.
In Jesus' name, I plead, stand by my side.

## Release

I'm frightened, God.
Soon I will be free, but I am terrified.
I have been removed from society for so long, Lord, and
I have few life skills from which to draw.
I am greatly aware that a small error or oversight when I
am free can quickly bring me back here.

Protect me, Father, from the evils all around me.
Guide me toward those who follow You.
Surround me with help and love and care when I need it.
Guide me, Father.
Show me the right path.
Stay with me on my journey that is soon to come.
Stay with me, too, for the rest of my life…
For I know I won't be able to do it without You.

## Fear of Freedom

Lord, would You believe I'm afraid?
How can I be afraid of *freedom*, Lord?!!
I'm due to be paroled very soon, Lord.
There are so many things to know—
From budgeting money to finding my way around
town on the bus system.
Where will I live?  How will I find work?
Unemployment is so high!
*How can I write a resume?*
Father, there are such challenges ahead.
I pray there will be someone to help me.
I pray for the strength to keep trying.
I pray for Your grace to keep me out of trouble.
*"Do not be anxious about tomorrow,*
*for tomorrow will take care of itself."*
Lord, help me to keep the rules of my parole.
Guide me to make wise choices with the challenges ahead.
I pray these things in the name of Your Son, Jesus.
Amen.

## Strength

My health is failing, Lord,
And I'm more alone than I have ever been.

I've been in and out of the hospital for weeks,
Having no contact with friends or family.
The system isolates us, tears us down, and separates us,
Lord.

Family doesn't even know we're ill
Until their letters are returned.
Since we can never receive phone calls,
Our friends don't hear from us, either.
We are often too sick to write,
And may not have stamps, anyway.

Strong people survive this system, Lord,
And I don't know if I am strong enough.
Lord, help me to keep believing…
That You care about me
And that You are at my side.

## Aging in Prison

Lord, I am old now. My hairline has receded and what is left is white. When I first came to this place, I was young and strong. Now, Lord, my muscles fail me, and I am unable to walk without help.

Many inmates around me are old, too. When I look around me, I realize that I have learned the meaning of compassion. Frailty and sadness surround me. We no longer receive visitors. My friends are now friends I've made within. Thank You for them, Lord, but I miss others. We are all tired, Lord, and need You more than ever.

Only Your love, Lord, holds me up. My body is weak, but Your loving arms support me. Now, Father, I live each day as Your servant. Bless me. Help me to show others, by my actions, that Your love is with us. Without You, Lord, I am nothing. With You, Lord, I find the courage to go on.

## Facing Death

Soon I will die. Father, I believe You have forgiven me because I do believe in You, and because I have asked You for forgiveness. But I am afraid.

Empty me of the anger, sadness, and regrets that still pull me down. Do not allow my trust in You to fail. Help me to draw on the strength of Your Son, Jesus, as He was slowly and brutally put to death. He died for sins that I committed—I get that now.

Surely with Your help, Father, I will be able to stand strong, as Your Son did. Indeed, You are my hope and my salvation...forever. Amen.

# Two

## He's Still My Brother

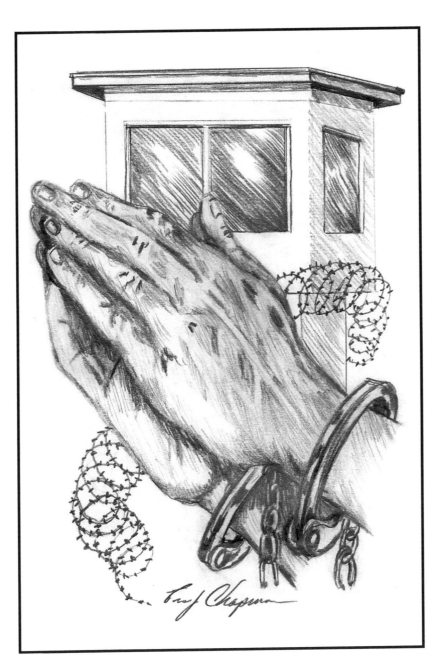

*Beyond the Chains*
Artist, Troy Chapman

33

## Hearing God Through Others

I am anxious, Father, and I feel so alone
I listen, but have to wonder if You hear me.
With every step forward, I take two back.
I try to stay positive and hopeful, but I'm still afraid.

When I feel like this, Lord, I've learned that I can find
You in my many brothers and sisters. You are inside every
one of them, Lord, and through every one of them You
speak to me.
Let me see You in everyone I meet today, Lord.
Let me hear Your words through someone else.
Maybe that someone else is afraid, too.

Thank You, Father, for my worldly family. You are so
good to me.

## For the Innocent

As I approach my release date, Father, I look around me
and see there are many here who have little hope of being
released.

It is a high price I've paid, Lord, but I've deserved all I
have gotten.

Lord, there are prisoners here who are innocent. I want
my release, Lord, but I also want justice for the innocent.

Look with favor, Lord, on those innocent souls.
Give them the strength to endure.
Help them to cling to the truth and comfort of a mighty
God Who knows the real score.

God, do not forget about them.

## He's My Brother

God, my bunkie is very slow.
He can't read, and he doesn't understand a lot of things.
Other prisoners make fun of him—
In front of him, and behind his back.

I try to look out for him, Lord,
But I can't always be there when he needs help.
Lord, how can I stop them from being so mean?
How can I make them understand that he just wants a friend?
How can I stop them from taking advantage of him?

He trusts and reaches out and only wants to please.
He does whatever anyone asks, often causing laughter, or
worse abuse.
Lord, I'm asking You to find a way to make them see the
good in him.
Watch over him, God.
Keep my bunkie – and others like him – safe from those
who would cause harm.

I ask this, Lord, because…after all…
He's my brother.

## Lessons Learned

I have learned…
Not to speak my mind because
I'll be called disrespectful.

I have learned…
Not to show compassion
because you get a "ticket" when you help someone
without being ordered to do so.

I have learned…
To think about the many ways I might not have been
caught,
Because I have so much time to sit and think.

Lord, take away my fears to do what I know is right.
Let me reach out to help my neighbor when he needs it.
Show me good ways to use the talents You have given me.

I know that I can do these things, Lord…
If only You will teach me and keep me strong.

I ask in the name of Your Son, Jesus.

## Hope

It is easy to give in to despair here, Lord.
There is so much evil all around.
So little hope.
I have lost everything, Father.
It is hard to go on, day after day.
I see many others, too, who are hurting—prisoners and
staff alike.

Help me to make the most of my time here, Lord.
Daily, I have chances to make someone's life just a little
bit better.
Father, show me more.

Your Son, Lord, reached out to those in need. Allow me
to spread Your loving kindness.
Guide me to find those who need to know Your love
today.
Let me help others to hope again.

## Friends

I had a letter from my brother today. I don't hear from him very often. I think his last letter came at Christmastime.

He mentioned that my good friend Freddie died last year. That was the first I'd heard of Freddie's death. No one had told me. We grew up together and were best friends. He became a teacher. I came here. We drifted apart. He'd write once in awhile, but, in time, there was little to say to each other. He had his life, and I'd lost mine. Now he is dead…and nobody told me.

Lord, help me to value the friends I still have. Friendship and brotherhood are treasures that You have blessed us with in this world. Don't let me ignore them or take them for granted.

## Not Alone

I am not alone.

Even though it often seems that way, I know that God is with me.

He knows all my thoughts and dreams and fears, and He loves me anyway.

Lately, though, I have been feeling that alone-ness again.

I don't want to be alone.

I'm *tired* of being alone.

I know God knows me, but nobody else does. My friends know only parts of me, and *no one* knows all of the same parts.

I want to be known.

I need to share who I am.

One way I can do this is by writing.

Another is by looking for Jesus in everyone I meet.

Father, help me to give enough of myself, wherever I can, so others will know me…and then through me, they can know You.

## Becoming Like Salt

I use salt to make my food come alive.
Jesus told His disciples they were "the salt of the earth."
They had the ability to make life better for others.

Lord, when I taste salt today,
May it excite me to look at others differently.
Do not allow me to ignore my fellow man.
Instead, Lord, let me offer a helping hand
Or kind word
When I see someone in need.

Lord, by reaching out to a person in need,
May I be salt to somebody's soul today as well.
Let my actions help to make Your word known.

In reaching out, Lord,
I know that You also know
That I am reaching out to You.

## My Brother's Keeper

I watched a man fall to the ground today.
I couldn't help him—I was in my cell.
As guards swarmed about him, they wouldn't help him.
Sadly, health care didn't come for more than half an hour.
I could only watch…watch and pray.

Those were the words of Jesus to the apostles in the Garden.
WATCH AND PRAY.
Instead, they slept.

Today, Lord, I didn't sleep.
Instead, I prayed for my brother.
Father, let me be my brother's keeper whenever
possible…
And when I cannot be, do not let me forget to pray.

## Beyond the Voices

God, that guy at the end of the block is very strange. Some days he's just fine and seems pretty normal. Then there are other days when he simply seems like another person.

He licks his lips a lot, and his tongue shoots out of his mouth now and then.

Sometimes you can hear him talking to himself—or maybe others. He says he hears voices. He says it's usually when he does what the voices tell him to do that he gets into trouble.

I've heard some staff say he's "mental." Others say he's schizophrenic.

I want to treat him like anyone else, Lord, but he scares me. Maybe it's because I don't understand.

Show me, Father, how to get past my fear and get to know this man. Show me how I can be his friend. I really think he needs one.

## Troubled

He sits and rocks
Back and forth
Most of the day.
I know this, because I can see him.
I see him from my cell.
But he doesn't see me...he only rocks.

Lord, guards think he's faking it,
But if he was faking it,
Wouldn't he stop and rest awhile?
I feel sad for him, Lord.
He can't help the way he is.

He also can't get help here, Lord.
The doc talks to him from outside his cell,
Everyone on the block can hear what is said.
Heck, I wouldn't talk either.

So many here need help, Lord,
And they don't get it.
What can I do, Lord,
To help these men?

## Change and Challenge

I ran into Ernie yesterday, Lord.
He looks so much older now!
But then, I guess I do, too.
He reminded me of the past, Lord.

When I first came here, I only cared about getting
through each day.
I'd fight and curse, hurting anyone who tried to hurt me.

But the years have passed and that man I once was is
gone forever.
I have found Your love and forgiveness, Lord, and that
means everything to me.

What do I have to show for my life, Lord?
I want to do something good with my life, Lord.

Father, lead me to some troubled soul,
For whom my words alone will make him choose life,
instead of death.
Let me help him get to know You, Lord.
Only then, will I not have lived in vain.

## Request for Meaning

Father, I have longed for a life of service...but I have been selfish and undisciplined.

I have longed to bring meaning to the lives of others, yet I struggle with the meaning of life for me.

Direct me, Lord, and build my confidence.
Help me to know that I can indeed help others.

Let me guide, or encourage, correct or caution.
Allow me to comfort the lonely.
Fill me with Your words, Lord, that I might serve others.

Let my service, Lord, bring someone peace.

## A Prayer for My Brother

Father, I am saddened and angry when I look around me. Older now—and I hope wiser—I know the wrongs that I have done, and the reasons I remain here. But I look around me, Father, and I see the young and the foolish. I see too many who are filled with their own egos. I see rebels who refuse to change. I see rage.

Father, lead these prisoners to You. Without You, Lord, I could never have survived the time. Father, lead my brothers to peace, as You have led me. I ask this in the name of Your Son, Jesus. Amen.

# Value

I used to think I was better than those around me.
I used to think I was "cooler" and smarter and stronger.

Here, behind these prison walls, I have been brought to
my knees.
Here, I've been treated just like everyone else...at times,
worse.
I've received no special treatment.
I have been unsure and afraid.

I've come to realize, Lord, that You love me—in spite of
my faults.
I've also learned to recognize who it is that I've become.
It is You I look to now, Lord.
I've learned that I have value.

Instead of feeling "better than" others, Lord, I look to *You*
to show me how to make *others* better.
Now it is You I see in them.
Father, help me to help them know that they, too, have
value in Your eyes.

# Three

I'm Blessed, in Spite of It All

*Shine, Jesus, Shine*
Artist, Troy L. Rienstra

53

## Early Christian

I used to have NO use for Christians.
I saw them as weak and wimpy pushovers.
I was the strong one who wouldn't take any crap.

Then one day I had to work alongside one.
The guard was yelling orders at us.
I wanted to talk back and give him a piece of my mind.
I'd probably have ended up in the hole, but this Christian
guy spoke softly to me.
He said we could get the job done if we just didn't get upset.
He kept me from opening my mouth, and that
was the beginning.

That day I learned I could respect someone who was both
quiet and strong.
Soon, this guy had me reading about Jesus.

Today I'm a very different person.
Today I even *like* me!  I'm not wishy-washy.
I'm still strong.  But now I'm strong for Christ.
I show it in how I treat those around me.
Thank You, Father, for leading me to You.

## From Weak to Strong

Angry. Hurt. Rejected. Alone.
I take on an I-don't-care attitude toward family and friends.
I build walls.
I think, "They can't hurt me if I don't let them."

That was before I learned about You, Lord.
At first, I thought You were a wimp to let them take You
without a fight, but then I realized how strong You really
were.
You hurt and You got angry,
But You held true to all You believed.

I'm strong when I admit my pain and anger.
When my family and friends do not believe me, or in me…
Even when they reject me as You were rejected
by mocking crowds…
I know, deep inside, that You still love me.

Thank You, Lord, for believing in me and for caring for
me when no one else does.
When I feel angry, hurt, or all alone, remind me, Lord,
that You are with me always.

## Hanging On

Lord, I have no family
And my friends are gone.
I fear that I will die here, Lord,
And not a soul will care.

Father, I look forward to the day
When I am no longer bound by bars and chains.
I know that I must serve my time
For all the wrongs I've done,
But I also know You have forgiven me
And that You'll welcome me
When it's my turn to come home.

Stay with me, Lord,
As I walk this lonely road.
Be my Source of strength
So I can make it to the end.

Without You, Lord, I have nothing.
With You…I have Life.

## Who is a Father?

A good father…
Takes care of, loves, calms, guides, encourages, teaches, is a role model, is sad when we disobey, still loves, still forgives, and always makes us want to be better.

Every kid needs a father.

Father, I pray for my brothers.
May all of us who need a father, Lord, seek, and find that Father…in You.

## Solitary Thoughts

Solitary.
Darker than a moonless night.
So quiet I could hear my heart beat.
Naked and cold, I was frightened, frightened and alone.

Alone, that is, except for You, Father.
Without knowing You, Father, the terror
Would have overwhelmed me.

I'm out now.
Thank You, God.
Thank You for keeping me sane.
That must be what it is like after death, Lord, when a soul
is without You—black, empty, and cold.

Father, keep me from ever having to return to that hell-
hole.
Lord, You are truly my Light and my salvation.
You do indeed light my path.
Walk by my side evermore.

## Blessed Healing

How can I redeem myself
In eyes of friends and family?
I've no excuse.
I did what I did.
No one forced me to do it.

Lord, I am no longer that same man.
I have changed and I have found You.
I've asked You to forgive me,
And You have.

I am blessed, and I am whole.
But those "outside" don't see me daily.
They don't believe and aren't convinced.

Lord, walk with me the rest of my life.
May my words and actions
Convince those who doubt me.
Most of all, Father,
Thank You for forgiving me.
May I never fail You again.

## Manna

A new man arrived on my block today.
Lord, he's so thin!
Then I remembered how,
Before my arrest,
I was homeless and on the run.
If I ate, it was often from somebody's garbage.
God, how I never want to be hungry again!

Father, I thank You for saving me.
My physical arrest saved my worldly life.
Learning of You, however, saved my spirit.

In You, Lord, I now know comfort,
And love,
And fullness
As I never did before.
With You, Lord…
I truly will never be hungry again.

## Reason to Go On

Father, I cling to You because You know how I feel.
You know what I need.
Some days I can be strong and self-sufficient.
Other days I struggle to go on.

On days like that, Lord, You bless me.
You find a way for something—or someone—to warm
my spirit.
One day You might allow me see someone being kind to
another.
On another day You bless me with someone showing
kindness to me.

Lord, thank You for these blessings.
Thank You for touching my life when I need it the most.

## Ever Present

Father, I wake knowing You are watching over me. I pray that You will walk with me throughout the day to come. Help me to be quiet when I want to argue. Make me patient when I find others irritating. As I think of all I will do today, I am confident that You will be near. Even in prison—perhaps especially in prison—I am often surprised to find Your hand at work.

When I lie in bed at night, I reflect upon the day. This morning You were with me when I listened to the fears of a new and frightened prisoner. This afternoon, You offered me a hand when I stumbled. Whether You work through me, or through someone else, I see Your loving touch at every turn.

Thank You, Lord, for Your protection, and Your love. Thank You for the times You use me, Lord. It is good to know You walk with me. Don't ever leave me, Lord. Continue to keep watch, oh Lord. I sing Your praises, Lord, each and every day. Amen.

# Insight

Lord, You've put me in my place.
I was ignored, and it made me angry.
I was put down, and oh, how that hurt. Someone else was
chosen when it should have been me.
Old feelings of anger and hurt were all I could feel.

But suddenly, Lord, I understood something.
I realized the hurtful things I've said and done to others
made them hurt and be angry, too.
I saw my pain and I saw theirs.
More important still, I saw that the hurt I've caused oth-
ers was not unlike the pain You felt at Your crucifixion.

Lord, make me recognize the pain my words can cause
before I speak them.
Never again let my actions cause pain.

Thank You, Lord, for caring about me in spite of my
hurtful ways.
Stay with me.
Allow me to heal wounds that I have caused.
It is Your love, Lord, that makes me long to be a better person.

# Belief

Father, You know our sicknesses without us having to tell
You,
But when we tell the doctors, they often don't believe us.
Doctors, nurses, guards all think we fake our complaints
so we can get drugs.
Granted, Lord, there are some who do that, but not all.
Father, You know all our needs.
You know when we hurt and when we don't.
When we come to You with every need, Lord,
Thank You for believing in us.
May we believe in You, oh Lord, more strongly
Every day.

## Lord, Let Me See

I was moved today, Lord, to a lower security level.
How wonderful it is to be in a room with a door, and not
a cell with a locking gate!
There are other "perks," too, Father.
I have longer yard time now.
I can come and go freely from my room.
I can call my family more often, and at different
times of day.
I even have a window that opens.
It overlooks the yard.

God, I never knew how much these things meant to me
until they were taken away.
Let me never take them for granted, ever again.

I thank You, Father, for Your many blessings. May I always see Your wonders, no matter where I am.

## Learning to Be Loved

Father, I have seen the eyes of men who abuse
drugs in prison.
Too often they are men with no conscience.
Too often they are men who feel they have nothing
to lose because nobody really cares.
God, I have felt desperate and alone, too.
It is a sick feeling in the pit of the stomach.
It makes you want to give up.

But now I know You, Lord, and You have blessed me
with family and friends who have reached out to me.
Lord, now I know the difference.
I am loved, and I can't help but love back.
I have seen Your blessings all around me.
The love You have granted me makes me want to love back.
I find myself reaching out now to family and friends.
Most especially, Lord, I find myself reaching out to You.

Thank You, Father, for loving me so much.
My cup overflows.
Use me...to let others know that You love them, too.
Amen.

## I'm Worth It

God, You have brought a special person into my life. This person cares about me and is willing to stand by my side. This person cares how I am treated. No one has ever done this for me before, Lord. I have always been alone— in my thoughts, and in all I ever did.

Father, this is new to me. I want to do right. I want to be worthy of the love that has been offered to me.

I want to please You, too, Lord. Show me the right path. Walk by my side, and guide me every day.

I didn't think I was "worth it" to anyone.

Thank You, Father. I sing Your praises for Your goodness to me. Help me, Father, not to fail again.

## Twisted

Things are twisted here, Lord.
It's strange how "bad" guys can become "good" guys.
There is a certain honor in our own ranks, a kind of
community when we see another wronged.

There's a guy in a cell near me who sees and hears
demons.
The guards laugh.
Some prisoners only torment him more.
Another man has constant pain and receives nothing for
it.
We can't always change it, Lord, but we see it.
Those with more courage sometimes speak out.

When we recognize evil and act against it, Father, we de-
light in knowing that we are now working for You.
It feels good.
Thank You, Father, for showing us right from wrong.
Strengthen us all to have the courage to <u>try</u> to right the
wrongs we see.

Thank You, Father, for blessing us in ways we never expected.

# Four

∽

## Recognizing the Past

*Lord, Please Watch Over My Family*
Artist, FreeRayGray

73

# If

God, can You hear me?
They tell me You're always with us.
I didn't know You growing up, Lord,
And I ended up here.

God, if I knew that You can really hear me
I'd tell You how much it means to me
To know there is Someone who loves me,
Who forgives me,
And Who wants the best for me.

I've been a very bad person my whole life, God.
If I knew You are really there,
I'd ask You if I can still make my life count for
something?

God, if You can really hear me…
If you're such a loving God…
Show me where to go from here.
Help me to see where, and how, I can make a difference.
Show me…if You really care.

## Quiet the Noise

God, it is not often quiet in here.
Gates clang until you stop hearing them.
Rap music blares from the cell next to mine.
Several televisions compete, each set to a different station.
Shouting and swearing goes on all day.
Every day.

Lord, the noise in my head goes on, too.
I'm restless and angry and I hear voices from my past.
Some days, I think of how things might have been different.
Other days I feel no hope at all.

Father, quiet the noise in my mind.
Let me realize that what's done is done.
Let me move forward in peace.
Help me to be sorrowful, Lord.
Grant me Your forgiveness.

Let the noise I make now, Lord, be joyful noise.
Give me the courage to tell others about You.
Let my words and actions become
My daily testimony to You.

76

## Reality for Tomorrow

Confined.
I am confined to this tiny space—
For the rest of my life.
I still can't believe it!
*How did this happen?*
I never thought of consequences.
God, had I known,
I'd never have chosen this!
Yet…I did.

Father, I'm begging Your mercy
And asking for Your help.
Let me accept my fate
And find a way to go on.
It may be the biggest challenge of my life, God,
But with Your help, Father,
I will find a reason for tomorrow.

## I Took a Life

I'm here for murder, God.
I say it was self-defense,
But the jury called it murder.
No matter what we call it,
I still took a life.

Father, I have a son.
I can't imagine how I would feel
If he were dead.
Forgive me, Lord, for taking life
From somebody else's son.
Forgive me for the pain I caused
To a father and mother somewhere.

Lord, You know that I am sorry.
Set my feet
To moving forward now.
Turn my life around.

I can never bring that life back,
But with Your help, Lord,
I can show others a better way to live.

## One of Them

God, I'm behind these bars because I cheated on my wife. She was so angry that she accused me of molesting our daughter. Never, Lord, would I hurt a child like that! While my wife had every right to be angry, it wasn't right for her to lie.

God, I know now what I should not have done, and I am very sorry for what I did. But I am lost now, Lord. I may not get out of here for a very long time, and no one cares. I'm here with robbers and murderers and drug dealers...but they are guilty and I am not.

Help me to not be afraid, Lord, and not to be too proud. Help me to accept that I am one of them now. Calm my fears and help me to use this time for good. Allow me to face the unpleasant truths about myself that I could not face before I came here. Let me leave here a new and better man, Lord.

# Regrets

My brother is dying.
We used to be really close, but time and place tore us apart.
Still seems like yesterday that we hung out and even
double-dated.
Suddenly time has passed, and now his life is nearly over.
He is just one of my regrets.

How foolish and stupid I was to make the choices that
got me here!
Father, I've missed so much.
I will never know what it means to be... a good brother...
a responsible son...to have a career and to be able to look
to the future...to have a family.

Lord, I know You have forgiven me, but that doesn't give
me the years back to change the past.
Do with me what You will, but let the rest of my days not
be lived in vain.
Guide me, Lord.
Use me only for good now.
Don't let me waste a single moment
Of the time I have left.

## Pre-Release

Everything I once had, Lord, is gone.
My wife left me and took my son, too.
I may never see either of them again.
My reputation is gone.
I have nowhere to call home, no money, no friends, no
self-respect, no dreams for the future.
I'm starting at the bottom now, Lord, and learning about
humility.

The parole board will meet with me soon, and I have
nothing better to tell them, Lord, than what I have
just told You.
I do want to leave here, Lord, but I know that will only
be the beginning of many more challenges.
I fear the future and a life without dreams.
Take me, Lord, to a higher place.
Raise me up from this depression.
Show me, and prepare me for, a new life in a new world.

Have mercy on this wretched soul, Lord.
Uplift me, and grant me one more chance at a life with
hope and a heart filled with dreams.

## The End is Near

I've been weakened, Father—
By medical needs that were ignored,
By an infection I received here, and
By uncaring staff who treat me as less than human.
I've lost friendships, Lord…close friendships.
I lost the love of my life.
I couldn't attend my mother's funeral.
My self-esteem is low,
My confidence is weak,
And my physical health is poor.
I hope, by now, I have paid for all of my sins, God.
I can't undo the past, Lord, but
Allow me now to help someone who is struggling.
I beg You, Lord, let my life count for something
In these, my final days.

## When I Fall

Lord, I made a promise to You yesterday that I would
never lie again….
But Lord…I did it again today.
I spoke the words almost without thinking.

I really meant it when I said I wouldn't lie again…I did.
But I failed You and I failed myself.

My Christian friends tell me that You will forgive,
over and over again.
I don't really understand that, Lord.
I would think You'd want nothing to do with me.

Lord, I'm so sorry that I let You down.
Why is it so easy to make up my mind, and once again,
so easy to change it?

Father, I will try again.
It seems like I'm always starting over.
Loving Father, stay with me.
Pick me up, I pray, each time I fall.

## No Chance to Say Goodbye

My mother died while I was here.
My sister died while I was here.
The man I cared for as an aide
Was taken to the hospital—and died—
While I was here.

*Lord, I never thought about things like this before!*

To not be at my mother's funeral
Because I was here...
Makes me ashamed.

My sister depended on me
Before I came here.
I let her down.

I never thought I'd get so close to the man
Whose wheelchair became a part of me.
Where was I, when he needed a friend?

I was here.
I never got to say goodbye.

# Five

≈

## Moving On

*Decisions to Come*
Artist, FreeRayGray

89

## Doubt

Lord, You have been my stronghold throughout my sentence. You have loved me when no one else has. You have heard my desperate pleas time and again and You have answered me. You have provided comfort when there wasn't any.

Yet, I am weak, Lord. Sometimes I doubt and wonder where You are. Then I convince myself that You don't care. I disobey Your laws and feel guilt or sadness or fear afterward. It is not till then I realize I've strayed from You.

Feed me, Lord, and make me strong. Remind me of Your blessings when I want to sin. Pick me up when I fall. Love me. Fill me...even when I don't deserve it...even when I turn my back on You.

## The Need for a Father

My ears perked up.
It wasn't so much the words that I had heard,
but more the tone of his voice.
This was the guy who locks a few doors down from me.
He was talking about his son.

What he said next could have applied to any one of us.
He said he didn't want to mess up because he wanted to
get out as soon as he could
to be with his son.

It was in that moment I saw his face—
kind of vacant, lonely, longing.
This man needed a father, too.
Whatever had happened to him in his past,
he was in need—now.

Father, I pray that You connect
This man and his son.
Reunite them.
Let their love be an example
Of the love You hold for every single one of us.

# Faith

I am longing
...for things I never had
...for the father who left when I was two
...for the mother who always tried to make me see the
  right way
...for a chance at the life I could have had
...and for a family who cares about me.

God, how can I keep going, day after day, watching
other prisoners be released when they've served less
time than I have, and when I have followed all the rules?

God, how can I keep going when all I can think about
is how things might have been?

God, give me hope and strength and—somehow—the
faith I need to make it through today—

Until tomorrow...when I will need You all over again
in the very same ways.

## Growing

Every day is a challenge, Lord.
But when I feel lost, You show me a path.
When I blurt out the wrong words,
You make me see how much those words hurt.
When I enjoy a dirty joke, or when I listen too eagerly
to gossip,
You remind me of how it feels to be talked about.
When I am shoved, and begin to shove back,
I see a picture of You turning the other cheek.
It is so easy to find evil all around me.
Lord, protect me in this place.
Give me strength to resist the temptations of drugs.
Help me to fight the desire to fight back.
Teach me not to argue.
Most of all, remind me to mind my own business.
I'm growing, Father, but I must be a slow learner.
Stay with me, Father...
Until I grow old.

## Discovery

My past continues to haunt me. I can't seem to shake it. I regret the pain I caused, the harm, the loss. I took what was not mine to take. I broke laws of both man and God.

I'm paying for my crimes against man now. I've asked God to forgive me...but I don't feel it. I've been reading the Bible. Some passages reassure me—for a short time. Others terrify me. But, today I found a passage I must live by:

**"He who believes in the Son has eternal life; but he who does not obey the Son shall not see life, but the wrath of God abides on him." (John 3:36)**

So it's not enough to just believe. I must obey Your words as well. Lord, I'll keep reading, and I'll try to do what You say. Maybe then, I'll feel Your forgiveness.

Strengthen me. Guide me. Every single day.

## Not in My Backyard

The free world fears me
And is revolted by what I have done.
They carry signs that read
"Not in my backyard!"
They want nothing to do with me
And they look on me as a monster.

Lord, I am repelled by my actions, too,
And I know I need help. But there is no help.
They don't know how to fix me.
Father, I dread my release.
I want to go home but I really have no home to go to
Because I am unwanted and unloved by all.

Lord, I beg for release from this cursed existence,
And I pray to someday be wanted and loved somehow.
Father, I cling to You. You are my only hope.
You are my strength, and
I am nothing without You in my world.

**"I can do all things through Him who strengthens me."**
**(Phil 4:13)**

## Murder

Jesus, the bible tells me that You spoke with a murderer
When You were hanging on the cross.
That should give me hope, Jesus,
That You will at least *hear* my words to You.
Yes, I took someone's life.
I took away somebody's child,
Maybe somebody's parent as well.

I barely knew my parents, Lord.
As a child, I longed for someone to love me.
*How could I ever have taken that away from anyone?*

Jesus, I'm behind these walls for a long, long time now.
Please talk to me—a murderer.
Show me how to live my life from this day forward.
I'm seeking, Lord.
I'm asking.
I'm knocking at Your door.
Tell me how to live my life in here.

## My Only Hope

Once I thought I had a future.
I would have taken over the family business.
My father—man, he was proud!
He kept telling everyone I would soon be the
new neighborhood grocer.
He'd been going to put me in charge,
and slowly retire. Then I screwed up.
I started hanging with a bad crowd.
The rest is history.
Now dad must keep on working.
Dad may never believe in me again.
I still don't have a trade to see me through.
*What will happen when I get out?*

I know—you could say I should have thought about
these things back then…but I didn't.
At the time, there was only the present.

Father, let me have hope for tomorrow.
Holy Spirit, give me wisdom to find my way.
Jesus, allow compassion to guide my steps.
You, Lord, are my only hope.

## Tree

I can see a tree from my cell window.
It was scrawny at first, but I've watched it grow
full and strong.
Lord, the beauty of Your creation overwhelms me.
Throughout the seasons You decorate this tree—
from tiny buds to full green leaves.
In the fall, their brilliant colors are inspiration for
all who care to see.

Lord, let me become like this tree.
Let Your rains quench my thirst.
Make my roots reach outward, growing stronger
every day.

May my actions stand out to others, as Your creation
stands out to me.
Let my colors inspire those around me to want to
know You by what they see in me today.
Father, I ask these things in the name of Your
Son, Jesus.
Amen.

## After the Parole Board

Today I faced the Parole Board. They asked questions, and I answered. I cried. Did they really hear my answers? Did they really "get" how different I am today? Do they have any idea how law-abiding I will be if I am ever allowed to leave this place? I wonder if they know how very much it would mean to me to be free to make choices once again...to make choices for the way I will live the rest of my life...to have family around me once again?

I am praying hard tonight, Lord. I am praying that these officials really heard my answers. I hope they were open to hearing my thoughts. I pray that they truly want to see me succeed on the outside, just as much as I want to be free. Lord, I hold my breath and pray with all my heart that this parole board is as much in Your hands, as my future is in theirs. Tonight, holy Father, hold me tightly in Your arms and do not let me go. I can barely breathe. Lead me, Lord...and lead them. Amen.

## The Power of Positive

Someone was kind to me yesterday.
And I was complimented today
On a job well done.
That felt really good,
But it was so unlike
What I've known my whole life.

I was beaten as a child
And told, time and again, that I was no good.
*I didn't know I was good at anything!*
How strange that I should come to prison
To learn good things about myself!

Lord, it's powerful to hear that I have value.
It gives me hope.
I know there are others like me.
Lord, help me to help others know this feeling, too.
Let me see the positive in myself.
Then let me see it in others.
Finally, allow me to let others know what I see in them
Because *knowing* you have value
Can turn your life around.

# Six

∽

## Knowing Whom to Trust

*Sole Asylum*
Artist, Nancy Jean King
105

## Coming Back

God, I need You in my life. I haven't let You in in a very long time. I remember my mom taking me to church when I was little, but then…our family fell apart and I drifted far away from You.

*God, I'm afraid to come back. I've been away so long.*

Some people think You are an angry, punishing God. But I don't think that's so. I still believe You love me. I want You in my life, Lord, and—deep down—I believe that You want me…

But I've been gone so long, Lord. *I don't know how to come back.*

Show me, God. Show me how to come back to You. Guide me. I'm probably going to need a road map, God. Put the right people in front of me, Lord, and let me take the straight road.

Lead me…until I find my way home.

## Fear

God, I know that only I am responsible for having gotten myself here. Had I only known! It is such a scary place. Here, I live among the mentally ill, the physically sick, and many who are angry and filled with evil plans. Just a look can, at times, be seen as a threat. Staff, too, cause me to be afraid. Some act as though they are better than us. Some seem driven to make every day a struggle.

Father, in here, little things become big things. My family doesn't understand. Yet, when so much of our former freedom has been taken from us, it is the smallest thing that often matters most. When an appointment is cancelled, or a mistake is made on my food tray, it is hard not to take it personally.

Father, calm my fears and those of other inmates. Help me to hold my tongue and to do nothing rash. Bless me with strength and help me to be patient. Help me to accept hardship and to use it as penance for my many sins. Lord, humble me. Let me learn to turn the other cheek.

## Detour

God, I started out okay.  What happened?
I was a pretty good kid.
I went to school.  I even got pretty good grades.
Then, I was walking home, past an apartment building
  where there was a drug bust.
I heard shots. Scared, I ran.
Suddenly, I was a suspect, then caught and arrested.
I had no money. The court-appointed lawyer didn't care
  at all,
And didn't fight for me.

I didn't do anything wrong, God, and yet, I'm here.

*Why here, God? Why me? Am I here for me, or for
  someone else, Lord?*

Father, protect me. Be with me. Teach me.
Show me what I need to see.
Then guide me…
To do whatever it is that is in Your plan.

## Desperate for You

It's been one of those days, God. It seems like nothing has gone right today. I woke to a fight between two prisoners. Then, in the chow line, the guy in front of me passed out. Later, I got a letter telling me my mom is sick. Finally, I called home. I was homesick, lonely and depressed, full of guilt and anger.

I don't like feeling this way, Lord. Help me to find a way to be positive. It's so hard to be positive in here, Father, but allow me to see and hear things that will make me think of You.

I need You a lot right now, God. Lead me from this unhappy place to higher ground where I can feel You at my side. *I really need to know that You are here.*

## Lifeline

I used to like to just sit by the river and fish.
I'd listen to the sound of the water and to the birds
calling.
I'd think about nothing in particular, or about whatever
was bothering me.

Here, Lord, it's just too noisy.
I can never be alone, and it is never quiet.
I'm frightened to be here.
I'm scared I may never get out of here—alive, that is.
Father, I can't think, and I can't focus on You.

But You know what I need, Lord.
I ask You to put it in front of me.
Help me to hear that You are near.
Show me how to survive this madness.

You are my lifeline, Lord, and I am forever in Your debt.

## Sole Companion

I feel so alone, Lord.
Nobody comes to see me here.
Friends and I have drifted apart.
My family wants to forget about me.

It's frightening here, Lord.
Constant noise drowns out my thoughts.
My every move, Lord, is watched by guards and
prisoners alike.
If I have something someone wants—guards or prisoners
—they find a way to get it.

So often, Lord, I feel that I am drowning.
Father, You are my Sole Companion.
Stay with me, and keep me afloat on this long, long
journey.

Only on You, Lord, can I rely.
Let my faith be strong enough to know that only You,
Lord, can see me through this journey to its end.

## Night Thoughts

At night, Lord, when things are quiet here, I do a lot of
thinking and a lot of feeling.
I think of how I got here, and of how one act changed my
life forever.
I think of people I have loved—family and friends I may
never see again.
I try to look to the future…but I can't see it.

I'm afraid, and I feel desperate.
I may never leave here, God!
I can't bear to think of spending the rest of my life here.
Still, it might happen.

God, I need courage…courage to face tomorrow and
every day after that.
Stay near me, Lord.
Help me to face another day.
I know that I won't be able to go on without You.

## Living with Passion

They say children learn what they live...
I grew up knowing hardship, depression, and despair.
No one had time for love.
Each day was a struggle to survive.
I learned about responsibility.
I learned about doing what had to be done.

Finally, in one desperate moment, I tried to take the easy
way.
I threw caution to the wind.
I only wanted the struggle to be over.
In one brief moment...I threw my life away.

Now, Father, I want to live again.
Free me from the past.
Allow me to look to a future.
Help me to find a passion for life, a reason to go on.

You loved us, Lord, with such great passion, that You gave
Your life.
Allow me the desire, Lord, to live passionately...
And let that passion be all for You.

## Condemned But Committed

What am I, Lord?
I am but a common man
Living a less than ordinary existence.
*Is this all there will ever be for me, Lord?*

Yes, I am paying for things I once chose to do, but Lord,
Don't let me have to keep on paying
For the rest of my life!
I have changed, Lord.
I've chosen You, Lord.

Lord, I'm begging You,
Light my path, and lead me to a better way.
May my way become Your way from this day forward,
And may my life become extraordinary
Because now I'm living it for You, God.

## Courage to Face Disbelief

They laugh at me, God,
Behind my back
And to my face.
They say I'm weak
If I believe in You,
And they say much, much worse.
But how can I *not* believe in You, Lord?
Every day here, I see hopeless people
In this pit of no hope.
I see the angry, tormented, unhappy, and withdrawn.
Yet, every day, Lord, I also see
Your hand at work.
Sometimes it's small,
But if I look for it, I can find it.
When I share these things, they tell me I'm a fool.
Help me not to care what others think, Lord.
Help me to keep on believing.
Father, give me courage to keep on telling
All about Your works,
And bless those who listen and hear
With Your awesome and uplifting grace.

## Voices

The voices tell me to do bad things, God.
They try to get me to hurt myself,
And when I do, staff get mad at me for listening to the
voices.

Pills help…they seem to keep the voices away,
But they don't always give me pills here,
And then the voices come again.
There is no one here to trust,
And no one here who cares.

God, You're all I have.
Take care of me.
Protect me.
I'm scared and I need You.

## Purpose

I've been watching a spider crawling up the wall.
He looks so full of purpose.
For him, he's probably covering a great deal of ground…
but he seems to have a destination in mind.

I wish that I, too, had a destination.
Here in prison, days go by, one after the next.
Sameness, dreary sameness, with no end in
sight.
Lord, I long to follow You, but I need to know
how to do this.
How do I follow You when those around me fight
and curse and steal?
Daily, it is a struggle to keep You uppermost in my mind.

Lord, lead me to more peaceful waters.
Help me to have hope for the days ahead.
Help me to find a purpose within this chaos.
Empty me of the needs *I* think I have, and leave me only
with a deep-felt need *for You.*

Father, show me the way.

## Clay

The man in the cell on my right committed murder. The man on my left sexually abused a child. I stole a car. The guy across from me sold drugs. We did these deeds. But did we ever think about spending years of our lives in prison, and having all of our freedom taken away?

I did not know You before I came to prison, Lord, but now I do. I never felt loved by anyone, Lord, and I didn't care about people or things around me. When I leave here, Lord, I want to live differently. I want to bring Your love to those who need it. I will respect You and my brothers and sisters, and their possessions. In fact, I will start today.

Since I have come to know You, Father, I have learned that You have love for all—for thieves and murderers alike. There are some here, Lord, who do not know You. Father, if You will, make me like clay in Your hands (Jeremiah 18:1-11) and mold me to do only that which pleases You. May I help those who do not yet know You, and help them to see. Mold me.

## At Your Mercy

God...if You're there...show me what to do.
I've been beaten...and raped...and beaten again.
Staff or fellow prisoners—it doesn't matter which—
Take advantage wherever, whenever they can...
In closets, in bathrooms, wherever a place is empty for a
few minutes.

Lord, God, I have been made to feel less of a person
and I no longer feel safe.
I'm frightened, God.  Can You help me?
I still believe in You, but I don't understand why these
things have happened,

Or why they have happened to me.
Protect me, Father, from those who would do it again.
Protect me, and show me how to live even one more day
Within these walls.

## Helpless

Father, I feel forgotten and so alone.
I'm in pain, yet nobody cares.
Perhaps this is my punishment
For the things I've done,
But, Lord, this shouldn't happen to anyone!
Love me, Father…for it seems no one else does.
Heal me, Lord, and make me better—that is my prayer.
However, if that is not Your will, then make me
Strong enough to endure my fate.
I can't help but remember the words of Your Son…
*Why have You forsaken me?*
Strengthen me with Your comfort, Lord,
For I am helpless without You.

## Alone and Forgotten

Father, I haven't had a visitor in years.
Even when a man has family, the prison doesn't tell them
that he is ill.
One by one, my hopes and dreams have vanished.
I have learned, Lord, that You are with me always,
But I feel so forsaken.
Help me to draw on the strength of Your Son, Jesus
As He was slowly and brutally put to death.
He died for sins that I committed—I get that now.
What a price to pay, my Lord and my God!
Surely I can stand alone as Jesus did.
Father, I beg of You,
Do not forget me.

## Scared

I am frightened, Father.
My health continues to get worse.
I tell my symptoms to the nurses and to the doctor, but
nothing seems to change.
I'm getting worse, Lord, and I don't know what to do.
My stomach is in knots.
I'm in pain.
My hands are shaking, and my tears are real.

Friends abandoned me years ago, Lord, and family barely
bothers to write.
It seems that I only have You now, Father.
At least, I pray that You are still by my side.
Don't leave me, Father.
I'm so afraid.
There is no way I can keep going without You.

## Desolate

I am sick and I am lonely.
I have no contacts on the "outside."
How frightened and lost I feel, oh Lord!
Simply feeling a hand on mine would be such
comfort.

Forgive me, Father, for being so wrapped up
inside myself.
I have learned, Lord, that You are with me
always.
Still, Lord, when I am feeling lost, somehow,
let me know that You are there.
I beg of You, Father, DO NOT forget me, ever.

## Nearing the End

Lord, I'm dying.
How I wish I'd lived my life differently!
How good it would be to have family or friends close by.
I'm frightened, Lord,
And I don't want to die alone.
Father, be with me as I make this journey to You.
Forgive me
And love me, regardless of all that I have done.
Take my hand, I beg You,
And lead me surely to the other side.

## Needing Help

Father, my health has failed.
I need help now.
I used to be able to offer my help to others,
but I no longer have the strength.
Now, my brother has to carry me.
Father, I don't like asking for help.
Is that pride?
I'm angry. Why does this have to happen to me?
I'm alone and scared, Lord…and dying.
Help me to face my fate with Your Grace.

## Death Row

I've been sentenced to die, Lord…and now, I wait.
I wait for "the system," and I wait for those who
would be happy with my death, to finally have their
way. I wait to see You.

Lord, I can't bring back lives that were taken. I can't
bring back family and friends who no longer believe in
me. I am alone—except for You, oh Lord. Therefore,
Father, I cling to You. You welcome me, even with all
my faults. You forgive my many wrongs.

Father, keep me strong to the end—in body and in
mind. If, by my words or actions, I may lead another
to You, make it so. Then lead me to greater challenges,
always for You. I ask these things in the name of Your
Son, Jesus, Who gave His life so I might live. Make it
so, Father. Let me make You proud of me at last.

## Why?

When I look around me, Lord, I'm reminded of many
who are no longer here.
Some have been moved to other prisons. Some released.
Others—bless them, Lord—have gone on to meet You.
Yet, I remain. *Why, Lord?*

*What do You want of me, Lord?*
Then…sometimes…I see a way to help…like advice for a
frightened youth, here for the first time, or a steady arm
for someone who is weak or ill.

Sometimes I see things that others don't…or maybe others just choose not to see them.
*Is that it, Lord?*
Okay, Lord…I'll keep trying.
Watch over me, okay?

Let me find my tiny spot in Your Great Plan, Lord, and
allow me to serve You.
Remind me, Lord, that when I see a need, I know I have
also seen my purpose.
With You beside me, I will make a difference.

## Bound

My wrists are shackled,
And there are chains around my ankles.
Though I was gravely ill in a hospital bed,
Still, I was chained to it.
The chains are an exercise in controlling anger, they say...
Humiliation, I say.
As soon as I become conscious of these feelings, Lord,
I am reminded of You.
*You* were mocked and spit upon,
*You* wore a crown of thorns,
*You* were made to carry a heavy cross, and
You did nothing to deserve any of that, Lord.
Lord, I'm guilty of much.
But I am paying my dues....
These chains, Lord, bind me to You.
They remind me to follow Your laws,
And that I am Your servant.
I need those thoughts, Lord.
*Un*bind me, Lord, from earthly discomforts
And bind me, instead, to You.

# About the Author

Seed for *The Prisoner's Prayer Book* was planted when the author joined a prison ministry group taking her inside one of Michigan's oldest prisons, joining Level V prisoners for worship services. Many were eager to read the selections, but many also struggled to read. Surprised by the eagerness, but struck by this realization, Louise began writing prayers. She says, "I met men who were eager for the merest connection of a handshake. No matter their outer bravado, I saw men who feared there was no one 'out there' who cared if they lived or died."

Louise is originally from Detroit, Michigan, has worked a variety of positions in social services, and is retired from Michigan's Department of Human Services. She lives now in Marquette, in Michigan's beautiful Upper Peninsula, and is helping to develop a support group for families of prisoners in her community. She is an advocate for prisoners and their families.

These "conversations" with God, written from the prisoner's perspective, are both simply written and "raw" with emotion. The prayers are *for prisoners*, the art work is *by prisoners*, and the book can be a gift from family, friends, or a faith community *to prisoners*. It is the author's prayer that they will make a difference in many lives.

Louise may be reached at...
email: 2inspire@chartermi.net
website: prisonersprayerbook.com

130